TEA AND TEA DRINKING

Claire Masset

SHIRE PUBLICATIONS

Published in Great Britain in 2010 by Shire Publications
Ltd, Midland House, West Way, Botley, Oxford OX2 0PH,
United Kingdom.

44-02 23rd Street, Suite 219, Long Island City, NY 11101,
USA.

E-mail: shire@shirebooks.co.uk   www.shirebooks.co.uk

A CIP catalogue record for this book is available from the
British Library.

Shire Library no. 600.   ISBN-13: 978 0 74780 794 0

Claire Masset has asserted her right under the Copyright,
Designs and Patents Act, 1988, to be identified as the
author of this book.

Designed by Tony Truscott Designs, Sussex, UK
and typeset in Perpetua and Gill Sans.

Printed in China through Worldprint Ltd.

10 11 12 13 14   10 9 8 7 6 5 4 3 2 1

COVER IMAGE

A group of elegant ladies enjoying a refined afternoon tea
in the 1920s.

TITLE PAGE IMAGE

Entitled *Over the Tea Cup*, this charming design for a
postcard was created by the American illustrator Harrison
Fisher in 1910.

CONTENTS PAGE IMAGE

By the early twentieth century, most large department
stores had their own tea rooms. This postcard shows
women enjoying tea at Maule's department store in
Edinburgh.

ACKNOWLEDGEMENTS

With thanks to Jonathan Barnicoat at Tregothnan Estate;
David Bond; Russell Butcher, Elizabeth Crawford and Nick
Wright at Shire; Nina Colls at Brown's Hotel; Noelle
DeSantis-Santangelo at Godel & Co. Fine Art; Kate
Eskdale, Richard Hopkinson and Alexis Tortolano at
Bonhams; Will Farmer at Fieldings Auctioneers; Adrian
Hellyer at www.teaantiques.com; Roderick Jellicoe at
www.englishporcelain.com; Gerrie Pitt at The Ritz; Ralph
Rudd; Philip Smith and Hayley Wooldridge at Mallams;
Stephen Twining and Helen Syme Nicholson at R. Twining
and Company Ltd. Special thanks to Alex and Gavin Toone,
Sarah Masset and Betty Gash.

Illustrations are acknowledged as follows:

David Bond, page 17; Bonhams Auctioneers, pages 21 and
34 (bottom); The Bridgeman Art Library, page 14; The
British Museum/The Bridgeman Art Library, page 9;
Brown's Hotel, page 43 (bottom); Country Life Picture
Library, page 16 (top); Mary Evans, cover image; Fieldings
Auctioneers, pages 32, 48 (bottom), 49, 50 (both); Godel
& Co. Inc., New York, page 38 (top); Adrian Hellyer of
www.teaantiques.com, pages 11 and 20; Lanesborough
Hotel, page 54 (bottom); Mallams Fine Art Auctioneers
(Copyright Hywel Lambert), pages 23 (both) and 37
(bottom); Peabody Essex Museum (USA)/The Bridgeman
Art Library, page 12; The Ritz, page 43 (top); Royal
Pavilion, Libraries and Museums, Brighton and Hove/The
Bridgeman Art Library, page 4; Twining and Company Ltd,
pages 18 and 24; V&A Images, page 22; Victoria & Albert
Museum/The Bridgeman Art Library, page 16 (bottom);
The Willow Tea Rooms, page 54 (top).

Shire Publications is supporting the Woodland Trust, the UK's leading woodland conservation charity, by funding the dedication of trees.

CONTENTS

INTRODUCTION

IT IS NO UNDERSTATEMENT to say that tea has had a huge impact on the British and their history. Since it arrived on British soil in the seventeenth century, its presence has been felt everywhere, from the country houses of the rich to the 'one up, one down' cottages of the poor. Although at first a luxury drink, affordable only by the wealthiest, by the twentieth century tea was one of the cheapest refreshments available. Over the last two hundred years, tea has become one of life's simple pleasures: from morning until evening, it revives the weary, relieves the thirsty and reassures those in need of solace.

The social history of tea and tea drinking tells us much about the British, including their culture, industry and sense of aesthetics. From fashion, decorative arts and even garden design to manufacturing, retailing and marketing, tea has made an appearance in almost every sphere of British life. At times it has even altered the course of history. Thanks to the replacement of gin with tea as a popular and increasingly affordable drink during the eighteenth century, people's life expectancy underwent a significant rise. During the nineteenth century, the temperance movement relied on tea as an attractive alternative to alcohol when persuading people to 'sign the pledge'. Some historians also believe, along with Winston Churchill, that tea was crucial in maintaining morale during the Second World War and may even have helped defeat Germany. Above and beyond these specific examples, tea has fundamentally shaped the British way of life. The 'nice cup of tea' has become something of an institution.

This enlightening book explains how – and why – this has happened. It paints a clear picture of tea's eventful history, highlighting some of its most absorbing or quirky aspects. For instance, you will find out about the curious invention of the tea bag, discover when tea gowns were worn and why tango teas became popular, and see how teapots varied from the functional to the fashionable. Ultimately, you will gain a vivid picture of how tea has affected the lives of so many people. More than a social history of tea, this is a celebration of Britain's favourite drink.

Opposite:
The Waitress
(1872), an oil
painting by John
Robert Dicksee.

A NEW LUXURY

WHERE DOES TEA come from? No one knows for certain. What we do know is that it is made from *Camellia sinensis*, an evergreen shrub or small tree with yellow-white flowers. Experts believe that the plant first appeared in the jungles of Eastern Himalaya, an area so rich in flora that scientists now describe it as a 'biodiversity hotspot'. Today, *Camellia sinensis* is cultivated in tropical or sub-tropical regions across the world, including China, India, Japan, Sri Lanka, Nepal, Kenya, Pakistan, Rwanda, Argentina and Australia. Since the early part of this century, it has also been grown in Cornwall. Blessed with a soil and microclimate similar to that of Darjeeling, Tregothnan Estate is the first commercial tea grower in the UK. Its teas are so fine that it supplies the luxury London store, Fortnum & Mason.

Perhaps because they are so obscure, the origins of tea drinking have over the centuries been explained by a variety of charming legends. One story claims that in 2,737 BC, tea leaves were accidentally blown by the wind into a herbalist's pot of boiling water. The man, Shen Nung, who also happened to be a Chinese emperor, found the taste so attractive that he shared his discovery with his people.

Before ever being consumed in hot water, it is likely that tea was chewed by early tribesmen. No one knows when and where people realised that it could be drunk as an infusion, but, during the Chinese Tang Dynasty (AD 607–907), tea drinking became more and more common throughout China, thanks in part to the publication in the eighth century of the first ever book on tea, the *Chajing* or *Classic of Tea* by 'the Sage of Tea', Lu Yu. This complete and intricate tea guide explained the mythological origins of tea, the different stages of its production, and how best to brew it, using up to twenty-five different utensils in the process. Appropriate tea wares and tea-drinking etiquette were also described in detail.

Over the years, the Chinese gradually became experts at manufacturing tea bricks – densely packed blocks of compressed tea. These valuable items travelled along the Ancient Tea Route, also known as the Southern Silk Road, a network of paths linking the Yunnan Province in south-west China to central

Opposite:
This late-nineteenth-century print shows the tea plant *Camellia sinensis*. Its leaves and leaf buds are used in the making of tea.

China, Tibet, Nepal, India and the Middle East. By the twelfth century, tea bricks were so ubiquitous that they were actually used as currency in many parts of central Asia – some were even scored, enabling them to be broken into smaller pieces and used as change. But it was only after 1391, when Emperor Hung-wu – founder of the great and long-lived Ming Dynasty (1368–1644) – requested the tea at his court to be in loose-leaf form, that this (now common) type of tea became more widespread.

It took a long time for tea to reach Europe, but thanks to the maritime explorations of the Age of Discovery a new global trade gradually emerged, involving the exchange of goods, such as silk, gold, silver, pepper, porcelain and tea. The Dutch and Portuguese started importing tea into Europe from about 1610 and in 1657 the first shipment of tea arrived on English shores. In the late 1660s the British started importing tea themselves through the English East India Company, on ships that took twelve to sixteen months to reach England. At first, tiny amounts were ordered: 143lb in 1669, rising to 5,000lb in 1678. This was the beginning of Britain's long and unbroken history of tea drinking.

Many believe that a Mr Wickham, an employee of the English East India Company based on the Japanese island of Hirado, was the first Englishman ever to mention tea in writing. Preserved in the India Office Records at the British Library in London is Wickham's letter, sent on 27 June 1615. In it Wickham asks a colleague in Macao (also known as Macau) to send him a pot of 'the best sort of chaw'. The first Englishman to write about tea whilst also residing in England was the famous diarist Samuel Pepys. He wrote of trying it for the first time on 25 September 1660: 'I did send for a cup of tee (a China drink) of which I never had drank before.' And, on 28 June 1667, he noted that, on coming home one evening, he found his wife making tea, 'which Mr Pelling the potticary, tells her is good for her cold and defluxions'.

Then as now, tea was seen as being both palatable and bestowed with special medicinal qualities. The very first tea advertisement published in Britain actually mentions its endorsement by doctors: 'That Excellent, and by all Physicians approved, China Drink, called by the *Chineans, Tcha*, by other Nations *Tay alias Tee*, is sold at the Sultaness-head, a Cophee-house in Sweeting's Rents by the Royal Exchange, London.' Published in the 23–30 September 1658 edition of the weekly periodical *Mercurius Politicus*, this was the first

Famous for recording the minutiae of his daily life in his *Diary*, Samuel Pepys was the first British person ever to write about drinking tea.

advertisement for a commodity ever to appear in a London paper. Also in the late 1650s, Thomas Garway (or Garraway), one of England's first tea and coffee retailers, published a document entitled *An Exact Description of the Growth, Quality and Vertues of the Leaf TEA*. In it, he stated that tea could help 'treat Headache, Stone, Dropsy, Scurvy, Sleepiness, Loss of Memory, Collick...' Anyone reading the document might have thought that tea was a cure-all. There is, however, an element of truth in this promotional pamphlet: as recent research has determined, tea does indeed have many health benefits, from helping to lower cholesterol levels and blood pressure and reducing the incidence of certain cancers to preventing tooth decay and stimulating the immune system. And as all tea drinkers know, tea also helps with concentration.

Strange as it may seem, tea was first available to drink in coffee houses. This can be explained in part by the fact that coffee was imported into England before tea. The earliest coffee house opened in Oxford in 1650, and it didn't take long before coffee houses appeared in London and throughout the country, offering men an ideal venue in which to drink and converse. While refreshing themselves with coffee, tea, chocolate, ale, wine or brandy, they could discuss affairs and catch up on news. By 1675, there were over 3,000 coffee houses in Britain. As the eminent social historian G. M. Trevelyan wrote: 'Every respectable Londoner had his favourite [coffee]

This seventeenth-century watercolour shows the interior of a London coffee house. It offers a reliable record of how tea was served in conical pots and drunk from shallow, handle-less cups.

9

Businessmen engaged in drinking, reading and lively conversation were a common sight in London's coffee houses, as this print of Lloyd's Coffee House vividly portrays.

house, where his friends or clients could seek him at known hours... In days before effective journalism, news could be most easily obtained at the Coffee House.' Soon, each coffee house developed its own specific clientele, ranging from businessmen and politicians to scholars, poets and clergymen – much like later gentlemen's clubs. Some of these establishments witnessed the start of successful and long-lived institutions. Most famously, Edward Lloyd's coffee house was the birthplace of Lloyd's of London, still today the world's leading insurance market.

Initially, the tea in these coffee houses must have been so unsavoury that one wonders why anyone actually drank it. Because it was taxed in its liquid form, and only once a day by a visiting excise officer, the tea had to be brewed early in the morning and reheated as and when required. Thankfully after 1689 tea began to be taxed in leaf form, which immediately stopped the habit of brewing all the day's tea in the morning.

Many coffee houses realised the commercial benefits of selling loose-leaf tea to their customers. This meant that men and especially women (who did not frequent the coffee houses) could enjoy the drink at home. Wealthy women subsequently initiated the refined custom of visiting each other for tea. These were elegant affairs involving dainty tea wares and furniture, such as teapots and cups, tea kettles, tea jars and tea tables. While servants laid out the table with the tea paraphernalia, the hostess brewed the tea herself and served it to her guests in her private sitting room, often known as a closet or boudoir. One such room can still be seen at one of Britain's best preserved seventeenth-century houses: Ham House in Richmond, Surrey, home to the Duke and Duchess of Lauderdale in the 1670s. It was in her Private Closet that the Duchess would keep some of her most treasured possessions, including her books and her tea. Here she would take tea with friends surrounded by lacquered, eastern-style furniture – an appropriately exotic setting for the enjoyment of what was at the time a highly exotic beverage. Visitors to Ham can still see the Duchess's delicate white teapot.

In the early days of tea drinking in Britain, tea leaves were kept in Chinese porcelain jars with lids or stoppers. Tea was served in tiny porcelain teapots and drunk from small handle-less cups (also known as tea bowls). All these items of Chinese porcelain were transported on the same ships as the tea. Being both water-resistant and heavier than tea, the porcelain was placed in bilges of ships where it acted as essential ballast, and could be sold on arrival at the docks. In the period 1684 to 1791, it has been estimated that about 215 million pieces of Chinese porcelain were imported into Europe.

When did the British start making their own teapots and tea

This late-eighteenth-century Staffordshire pearlware tea canister has been designed to imitate a valuable Chinese export blue-and-white porcelain jar. From the eighteenth century onwards, countless variations of blue-and-white ceramics were produced by British potteries.

During the seventeenth century and for most of the eighteenth, tea cups (or bowls) were handle-less, as is this New Hall tea bowl from 1795. Handles started appearing in the 1750s, but it took over fifty years for them to become the norm.

wares? As we shall see in the next section, the British fascination for making tea wares really took off in the eighteenth century. However, one of the first English teapots was made out of silver in about 1670. It was given to the directors of the East India Company by Lord Berkeley. Its inscription reads: 'This silver tea Pott was presented to the Committee of the East India Company by the Right Honourable George Lord Berkeley of Berkeley Castle.' This simple yet elegant item, similar in style to contemporary coffee or chocolate pots, is in the collections of the Victoria and Albert Museum in London.

The British always favoured adding sugar to their tea. Milk, on the other hand, didn't appear in the drink until about 1720. The British habit of taking tea with milk probably originated in France in the late seventeenth century. It is strange to think that nowadays the French prefer to drink their tea without milk, and often accompanied with a slice of lemon.

Tea drinking in the seventeenth century was very much a royal and aristocratic pursuit. Many experts credit its popularity at the English royal court to the arrival in 1662 of King Charles II's Portuguese wife, Catherine of Braganza. Tea was already a popular beverage in Portugal and Catherine herself had been enjoying it since her youth. She continued drinking tea after

A nineteenth-century painting shows items of porcelain being carefully packed. The man on the left is pouring sand into a box to stop the bowls from getting broken during transit.

This fashionable mid-eighteenth-century lady is sipping her tea from a spoon while she waits for the drink to cool down.

settling in England and helped establish a fashion for the drink. The appearance of tea drinking in Scotland has been partly attributed to Catherine's sister-in-law Mary of Modena, wife of King James II (and James VII of Scotland). It was she who in the 1680s introduced the habit at Edinburgh's Royal Palace at Holyrood. Subsequent monarchs William and Mary and Queen Anne (and, much later, Queen Victoria) were also keen tea drinkers.

Although tea leaves were still very expensive, by the end of the seventeenth century more and more wealthy families were enjoying tea as part of their daily routine. At breakfast, tea, coffee or chocolate were often served instead of the usual beer or ale. During the day, tea was drunk in the coffee houses or at home by women, and, in the evening, aristocratic men and women retired from the dinner table to have tea. As we shall see in the next chapter, during the course of the eighteenth century tea drinking began percolating down to a much broader section of society.

TEA IN THE EIGHTEENTH CENTURY

IN ABOUT 1700, one pound of good-quality tea cost a skilled craftsman approximately three weeks' wages. Fuelled by heavy taxes, the price of tea remained high throughout the first half of the eighteenth century. It was only in 1745, thanks to a reduction in duty from 4s to 1s, that tea drinking started to become more widespread. Even more significant was the Commutation Act of 1784, introduced by the Prime Minister, William Pitt, which reduced the tax on tea from an astounding 119 per cent to 'just' 12.5 per cent. Nothing highlights the increase in Britain's tea drinking more clearly than the rise in tea imports from the English East India Company – from £14,000 of tea in 1700 to £969,000 in 1760, and £1,777,000 by 1790 (a far steeper growth than the rise in the rate of inflation). Some historians claim that it was because the English East India Company imported such vast quantities into England that we became a nation of tea, rather than coffee, drinkers. Certainly, while demand for tea augmented imports, rising imports also created more demand.

Even before tea became more affordable later in the century, the British – already hooked on the beverage – found ways to get hold of it more cheaply. The quantities of tea smuggled into the country, before taxes were significantly reduced in 1784, were vast. Experts estimate that during the course of the eighteenth century over 7 million lb of tea were smuggled into England each year, compared to just 5 million lb of legal tea. Even more surprising is the fact that so many people bought smuggled tea fully aware of its illicit nature. Some respectable members of society, including clergymen, went as far as collaborating with smugglers.

That the British went to such great lengths to be able to enjoy their favourite new beverage is also brought to light by the 'popularity' of adulterated tea. Used black tea leaves were mixed with some bizarre adulterants, including ash, sloe or hawthorn leaves, and then pressed, dried and roasted to create an ersatz tea. Although less palatable than real tea, it filled a gap in a newly tea-craving market. It also went some way to helping rid the nation of its gin craze, the cause of so many ills – from crime, promiscuity and poverty to illness and death – during the first half of the eighteenth century.

Opposite: Notice the fashionable blue-and-white porcelain and the tiny tea cups in this lively eighteenth-century scene.

The elaborate tea alcove in the Chinese Room at Claydon House in Buckinghamshire. Dating from the 1760s, this was one of the first rooms designed for the consumption of tea in a British country house.

For the most part, however, tea drinking in the early to mid-eighteenth century was still very much a wealthy pastime, its practice a symbol of affluence, status and good manners. For the mistress of the house, the ritual gave her an element of power and independence: keeping the key to the caddy safely around her waist (away from snatching servants' hands), it was she who brewed and served the beverage, taking centre stage in an important social custom.

As tea drinking became ever more popular amongst the rich, some country house owners went as far as remodelling their homes to provide a dedicated tea-drinking room. Dunham Massey in Cheshire is one such example. Its Tea Room was used for the after-dinner drinking of tea, served in a splendid silver service. Similarly, in the 1760s Claydon House in Buckinghamshire acquired its Chinese Room: a private room where family members could sip tea while seated in a cosy alcove modelled on a Chinese tea house. At the same time, some Elizabethan and Jacobean outdoor banqueting houses, originally designed for the enjoyment of a pudding course after a formal meal, were transformed into tea houses. Others – such as the dual-purpose Tea House Bridge by architect Robert Adam at Audley End in Essex – were created from scratch and placed in newly fashionable landscaped gardens.

A Family of Three at Tea (c. 1727) by Richard Collins. During the eighteenth century it was not uncommon for well-to-do families to be painted drinking tea. The resultant portrait highlighted the family's wealth and good taste.

One of the world's most luxurious tea houses can be seen in the grounds of Sanssouci Palace, Frederick the Great's eighteenth-century summer residence in Potsdam, near Berlin. This elaborate building, a glorious mix of rococo and Chinese decoration, features extraordinary gilt columns in the shape of palm trees and groups of life-sized oriental figures, one of which is pouring tea.

By the end of the century, both rich and poor were enjoying the pleasures of tea. After a visit to England in the 1780s, the French Duc de La Rochefoucauld wrote: 'Throughout the whole of England the drinking of tea is general... Though the expense is considerable, the humblest peasant has his tea twice a day like the rich man.' During his travels, the pioneering social commentator and author of *The State of the Poor* (1797), Sir Frederick Eden, noticed: 'Any person who will give himself the trouble of stepping into the cottages of Middlesex and Surrey at meal-times, will find, that, in poor families, tea is not only the usual beverage in the morning and evening, but is generally drunk in large quantities at dinner.'

Country house owners keen to enjoy tea outdoors commissioned special tea houses, such as this neoclassical and dual-purpose Tea House Bridge designed by Robert Adam for the gardens at Audley End in Essex.

An early twentieth-century painting showing the Twinings shop in the Strand, which one can still visit today.

While the poor may not have written about their passion for tea, one man who perhaps more than any other captured the growing importance of the drink was the famous lexicographer Dr Samuel Johnson. Describing himself as a 'hardened and shameless Tea-drinker', Johnson once amusingly said: 'You cannot make tea so fast as I can gulp it down.' His kettle 'scarcely had time to cool, who with Tea amuses the evening, with Tea solaces the midnight, and with Tea welcomes the morning.' Without tea, would Johnson ever have produced his famous *Dictionary of the English Language?* Another great man, the Duke of Wellington, liked to sip tea made from his Wedgwood teapot while on the battlefield because it 'cleared his head'.

As tea consumption rose, so did the number of places where one could enjoy it. From the very beginning of the century, coffee houses and tea merchants proliferated. The most famous of these was without doubt the Twinings Golden Lyon shop on the Strand. Opened in 1717 by Thomas Twining, it was London's first tea shop. Three hundred years on and it is still selling tea, making it the oldest London shop still trading from the same site. Thomas Twining became famous for his tea blending, paving the way for the creation of such well-known blends as Earl Grey (invented by Jacksons of Piccadilly in the 1830s and named after Charles Grey, 2nd Earl Grey, British Prime Minister between 1830 and 1834) and English Breakfast (which, perhaps surprisingly, was created in only 1933 by Twinings).

In *A Social History of Tea*, tea expert Jane Pettigrew explains how, much like today, London's eighteenth-century office workers were able to buy tea from special 'breakfasting huts' on their way to work. An advertisement from a contemporary London newspaper reads: 'This is to give notice, to all Ladies and Gentlemen, at Spencer's Original Breakfasting Hut … may be had every morning, except Sundays, fine tea, sugar, bread, butter and milk.' Tea, also served with milk, bread and butter, could be enjoyed in the popular pleasure gardens, such as those at Vauxhall, Ranelagh and Marylebone. These early 'theme parks', of which there were over sixty in London, featured verdant walks, concerts and other performances, outdoor games, boat rides, as well as masquerades and firework displays in the evenings. Not confined to London, pleasure gardens also appeared in towns throughout the country, including Bath, Norwich, Liverpool, Newcastle and Birmingham.

The first and best-known of London's pleasure gardens was Vauxhall, but Ranelagh Gardens in Chelsea was without doubt the most spectacular. For half a crown, visitors could enjoy tea, coffee, bread and butter, explore the elegant gardens, perambulate the gravel walks lined with yews and elms, and experience the spectacular Rotunda. At over 150 feet in diameter, this was a sight to behold. Resembling somewhat the interior of the Pantheon in Rome, it featured a huge domed ceiling hung with crystal and gilt chandeliers lit by thousands of candles. Much like a theatre, its circular wall was lined with boxes (from where visitors could enjoy concerts) with refreshment tables (featuring the ubiquitous tea) placed at intervals. In the centre of the Rotunda, an elaborate colonnade housed a huge fireplace for use on cold evenings and during the

Eighteenth-century families spent many a leisurely hour drinking tea and enjoying the verdant surrounds in Britain's newly fashionable tea gardens.

MARYLEBONE GARDENS. (*From a Print of 1780.*)

At Marylebone Gardens, visitors could enjoy the sights and sounds of firework displays and concerts (from the bow-fronted orchestra, shown on the right), promenade along tree-shaded walks or drink cups of tea in one of the latticed alcoves (shown at the back of this print).

19

A popular blue-and-white design has been used on this New Hall tea bowl and saucer from about 1795.

In the eighteenth century it was very common for teapots to have a matching stand, as can be seen in this Caughley teapot and hexagonal stand from 1785.

winter. The fashion-conscious would gather here to show off their finest outfits and engage in polite conversation or a spot of gossip.

While the higher echelons of society generally converged in the large pleasure gardens, smaller versions of these – known as tea gardens – served the needs of the middle to lower classes. Situated mostly in the suburbs of London, they offered an attractive day out for local families. Here, visitors would drink tea in specially designed tea rooms or in shady arbours, stroll amongst the lawns and beside lakes, and maybe enjoy a game of bowls. Some of these gardens had delightful names, such as Adam and Eve's Garden, Merlin's Cave, Finch's Grotto and The Three Hats!

Unsurprisingly, the eighteenth-century rise in tea drinking coincided with an increase in the availability and variety of tea wares and furniture, as consumers demanded ever more elaborate and specific utensils to satisfy their new habit. Top of the list were teapots, tea jars and canisters, tea bowls and saucers, tea kettles, sugar basins, milk jugs and teaspoons (often numbered so that the hostess could remember which spoon belonged to which guest when she was re-filling tea bowls). But there were also sugar boxes, tea trays, teapot stands, tea plates, tea tables, spoon trays and boats (for wet teaspoons), and wooden or silver tea caddies (which increasingly replaced Chinese porcelain tea jars). At the same time, matching tea sets were becoming more and more available; wealthier consumers could even order their own bespoke – or at least tailored – sets of matching Chinese porcelain.

European potteries couldn't help noticing the booming trade in Chinese porcelain and they soon started producing large amounts of tea-related items in the hope of capitalising on this growing market. So much so, in fact, that in England the manufacture of ceramic wares became a highly significant part of the nascent industrial economy. This was particularly true of the Stoke-on-Trent and North Stafford area, an area which became known as The Potteries and was home to Wedgwood (established in 1759), Spode (1767), Minton (1793) and, slightly later, Royal Doulton (1815).

For decades, European potters had been racing to discover the secret to making porcelain: the translucent, highly delicate but also heat-resistant

An elaborate George II tea kettle and stand by Richard Gurney and Co., London, from about 1740.

material which the Chinese had been making for centuries. The German firm of Meissen developed its own version, called hard-paste porcelain, in 1709, but it was not until the 1740s that the British started producing what is known as 'soft-paste' porcelain. The Chelsea factory was the first British manufacturer of this type of porcelain, followed by Bow (1747), Derby (1750) and Worcester (1751), among others. While some firms concentrated strictly on porcelain production, other potteries focused on different materials and new techniques. The influential Thomas Whieldon, one-time business partner to Josiah Wedgwood and teacher of Josiah Spode, is particularly remembered for his agate ware, popular between 1725 and 1750. Named after the agate stone, it featured two or more coloured clays which combined to create streaks or veins reminiscent of smoke or cloud patterns.

Josiah Wedgwood, arguably the most innovative and successful potter of the eighteenth century, had a strong impact on the history of ceramic tea wares. He was so meticulous that each of his teapot designs – which ranged from quirky cauliflower shapes to classically inspired scenes – was personally tested by his wife before going into production. In the 1750s he became famous for his 'Creamware', a pale-coloured earthenware with a smooth glaze, which in the 1760s became known as Queen's Ware, after Wedgwood had given Queen Charlotte a Creamware tea set. In the 1760s and 1770s, Wedgwood went on to develop a range of different ceramic materials, including the famous Jasper Ware, which is still manufactured today.

Of even greater importance than the work of any single British potter to British tea wares was the end of Chinese porcelain imports by the English East India Company in 1791. This – coupled with the invention of the hard-wearing, pure-white and cheap-to-manufacture bone china in about 1800 – helped pave the way for a flood of tea-related ceramics in the nineteenth century, the subject of our next chapter.

This mahogany tea table was designed to accommodate a whole tea set: cups and saucers fit perfectly in the circular outer panels, while the teapot, stand, milk jug and silver sugar nippers have their place in the centre. The set was made by the Chelsea Porcelain Factory and dates from the 1760s.

Left: A George III silver tea caddy with caddy spoon by T. Phipps & E. Robinson, London, 1791.

Wooden caddies were extremely popular in the eighteenth century. The locks on each of them ensured that valuable tea was not stolen.

TEA DEMOCRATISED

IN ABOUT 1805 Josiah Spode perfected a revolutionary type of porcelain containing animal bone ash. Strong, translucent, pure white and cheap to produce, bone china became the material of choice for teapots and related tea wares. Its affordability meant that even the rising middle classes could now afford a 'proper' tea service, while the rich and fashion-conscious could indulge in a new set every few years.

Victorian decorative arts are often described as eclectic, displaying an astonishing number – sometimes even a mixture – of styles, such as neoclassical, gothic, rococo and baroque. Teapots were no exception and came in an array of shapes and colours, decorated with either patterns or sculptural motifs, or both. Some were so 'over-embellished' that one wonders how they were actually used. But in this new age of consumerism, choice – whether garish or tasteful – was the order of the day.

Further technical innovations helped bring about significant changes to tea wares. Refinements in transfer printing (first developed in the 1750s) meant that images could now be applied to a curved surface, such as that of a teapot, as part of the mass-production process. So, while at the top end of the market, teapots and related items may still have been hand painted, transfer printed wares offered an affordable alternative for the middle classes. Similarly, the technique of electroplating, perfected by Elkington & Co. in the mid-nineteenth century, meant that teapots that looked like solid silver – but were in fact plated – could be bought for about a third of the cost of silver ones. This was an ideal choice for an 'aspiring' household keen to make an impression.

While tea wares became cheaper thanks to advances in technology and the growth of mass-production, tea itself became more affordable during the course of the nineteenth century, thanks mainly to the establishment of British-run tea plantations in India.

The British had relied on the Chinese for tea, but one significant event was to highlight the fragile, and also morally corrupt, nature of the tea trade. This was the Opium War of 1839–42. Its roots go back to at least 1758, when

Opposite:
By the end of the nineteenth century colour advertising was fairly common, as this 1899 Twinings advert beautifully demonstrates.

As this Nectar Tea postcard shows, elephants were used in tea plantations. Duties ranged from clearing of land for cultivation to carrying loads of tea.

Tea plants were grown to waist height to make harvesting easier. In its wild form, the tea plant develops into a large tree. Only the freshly grown top leaves were plucked.

Parliament gave the East India Company the monopoly of the opium production in India. For the next hundred years or so, the British grew vast amounts of opium, mainly in Bengal, and illegally exported it to China. While this important source of revenue helped fund Britain's tea-drinking habit, opium addiction spread across China like wildfire. By the 1830s the country had about three million opium addicts. The Chinese Government decided that drastic measures were needed to stop this 'epidemic', so it burned a year's supply of opium (about 20,000 chests) on 3 June 1839. Horrified, the British declared war and the Chinese reacted by placing an embargo on tea exports. Although the Opium War ended with the defeat of the Chinese in 1842, by then it had become clear that Britain needed to grow its own tea to free itself from its dependence on China.

A few years before the war, steps had already been taken towards growing 'British' tea. In 1834, the East India Company established its first Tea Committee. Its aim was to create 'a plan for the establishment of the introduction of tea culture into India'. A few years earlier, the British had taken over Assam in north-east India: it was here, in 1835, that tea plants were first found by Englishmen. How ironic it is, then,

LEAF SPREAD TO WITHER

For Nectar Tea Co.

Once plucked, the tea leaves were spread onto racks and left to wither for up to twenty-four hours. This was just one of many stages in the tea production process, which could also involve rolling, fermentation, firing, sorting and packing.

that instead of focusing on growing Assam tea, the British decided to introduce Chinese tea plants into Assam, in the mistaken belief that these would produce better tea. Gradually, they realised their mistake and by the late 1880s all tea grown in Assam was from the region's native tea plant, now called *Camellia sinensis var. assamica*.

Assam became a huge tea plantation. British tea speculators bought plots, hired 'coolies', cleared the land, cultivated the tea plants and collected the profits. As Claire Hopley explains in *The History of Tea*: 'India tea growing was like the enormous factories in Britain: bushes were planted in long rows marching over hillsides and tended by armies of workers. These economies of scale made Indian tea cheaper than Chinese, which was grown in family plots.' The principles of discipline, efficiency and division of labour that had been successfully applied to the manufacturing industry in Britain were effectively transferred to tea cultivation in India.

Labourers were hired by 'coolie catchers' and forced to sign seven-year contracts, which virtually enslaved them. While British staff were housed in comfortable bungalows, workers often lived in cramped and unhealthy conditions. Huge tea factory buildings were built for the processing of tea leaves. Assam tea plantations were so successful that commercial tea estates were soon established in other parts of the British Empire, particularly in Darjeeling (in the early 1850s) and Ceylon (in the 1860s).

These new British-run plantations had a huge impact on tea drinking in the United Kingdom. In 1889 Indian tea exports to Britain overtook Chinese tea exports for the very first time, thereby crushing the Chinese monopoly. A mere ten years later, Indian exports were fourteen times higher than Chinese exports (219,136,185 lb compared with 15,677,835 lb).

TEA FACTORY AND COOLIE DWELLINGS

Entire 'villages' were erected around the tea plantations. The tea factory, used for the processing of tea leaves, is the large white building.

The tea produced in India and Ceylon was mainly black, whereas Chinese tea was both black and green. Over the course of the nineteenth century Britain became – and still is today – a nation of black tea drinkers. At the same time, tea, since it was now manufactured as an industrial product often in huge plantations, became cheaper and more widely available. Some tea merchants, including Thomas Lipton, went as far as buying their own tea plantations. By cutting out the middleman, they were thus able to reduce prices. In 1890, Lipton bought four tea estates in Ceylon, after which he adopted the slogan 'Direct from the Tea Gardens to the Tea Pot', which appeared on colourful tea packets and advertisements. He made sure his name, which soon developed into a successful brand, was placed on as many items as possible, including the wooden boxes of tea carried by the elephants and the tea pickers' baskets.

Another element relating to these new tea plantations may also have had a significant impact on the British tea drinker. This was the fact that tea, now produced in British colonies, had become, in the eyes of some at least, a truly 'British' drink. Gone were the days when tea was an exotic commodity; it was now a British product and part and parcel of the British way of life. So much so, in fact, that the nation's tea consumption rose from 23,730,000 lb in 1801 to 258,847,000 lb in 1901 – higher than the phenomenal population increase of nineteenth-century Britain.

In the 1840s, the appearance of tea clippers added a fresh excitement for the tea-drinking public – and this may also have helped boost consumption. Replacing the bulky East Indiamen, these sleek, super-fast ships, each one capable of carrying over 1 million lb of tea, cut the journey time from Canton to London from 200 to about 120 days. When the clippers set sail in May or June with the new season's tea, they immediately entered into a frenzied race, as the first tea to arrive in London would fetch a much higher price than later shipments. British newspapers enthusiastically reported on the race, bets were taken over which clipper would arrive first, and in the autumn crowds gathered at the docks to wait for the ships. Such was the cachet of winning the race that some captains barely went to bed during the three- to four-month voyage, opting instead to catnap on deck. The days of the tea clipper came abruptly to an end with the opening of the

Thomas Lipton was a canny self-publicist, using every opportunity to flaunt his brand, as can be seen here in these two promotional postcards.

29

THE GRAPHIC 53

Suez Canal in 1869. Soon thousands of tea-carrying steamships plied this new route between the Far East and Europe via the Mediterranean.

Back in Britain, new commercial developments were starting to affect the tea-drinking market. The growing importance of packaging, advertising and retailing – what is now referred to as the four Ps of marketing: product, price, placement and promotion – was an almost inevitable consequence of the industrial boom. Gradually, the selling of products became a sophisticated 'game' and the growing breed of specialist tea merchants was quick to learn its rules.

John Horniman was one of the earliest retailers to see the potential of this approach. In 1826 he was the first to sell pre-weighed, pre-packaged and labelled tea. This had a number of advantages. While the tea was guaranteed to be unadulterated, its weight was clearly marked on a foil-lined packet which kept the leaves fresh and safe from dirt. Another advantage was that Horniman could use the packet, together with targeted advertising campaigns, to promote his name. Horniman's Tea soon became a recognisable and reliable brand.

Boasting that you had paid the biggest weekly tea-duty cheque was a great way of affirming your position at the top of the tea market. Both Lipton and Mazawattee used such news in their advertisements to bolster sales.

Mazawattee often used the image of two ladies drinking cups of tea in its advertisements. The younger lady is enjoying a spot of tasseography, the practice of reading tea leaves.

Other merchants followed suit, each promoting their own 'unique selling point'. In the 1840s, businessman John Cassell developed a successful tea business focusing mainly on the working-class market. He flooded the industrial north with his affordable 'Tinfoil Packages, from One Ounce to Once Pound'. At the time, his was the only tea that could be bought for just a shilling. Cassell later invested in a printing press, creating his own tea labels and printing his first magazine, appropriately named *Teetotal Times* from which he built a publishing business.

At the end of the nineteenth century, Lipton's developed a successful brand based on catchy slogans, bright packets and effective advertisements. They became famous for creating blends specially suited to the different regions of Britain, using the slogan: 'The perfect tea to suit the water of your town'. Lipton's famous Yellow Label, developed in the 1890s, was an instant success and, although it is no longer available in Britain, it is still sold in Continental Europe, North America, Australia, the Middle East and Asia.

One of the most successful tea companies of the nineteenth century was Mazawattee, founded as Densham & Sons in the 1870s. Their name is a combination of the Hindi word 'mazza', meaning 'pleasure' or 'luscious', and the Sinhalese 'vatta', meaning 'garden'. To develop its brand, the company decided to show an image of an old woman and a young woman enjoying a cup of tea on their advertisements. This clever device was particularly

From the 1880s, Lewis's of Liverpool (here shown in an early twentieth-century photograph) started selling its own brand of affordable teas.

Lewis's, Liverpool

successful. Mazawattee, along with other tea companies, also featured images of the royal family, especially Queen Victoria, on their products and advertisements. This certainly helped add a certain prestige to their name. During the twentieth century, tea companies continued to use people or characters to represent their brand. Brooke Bond's PG Tips chimpanzees were perhaps the most famous: introduced to the British public in 1956, they were familiar faces on television until 2002.

Tea was seen as such a marketable commodity that a few businessmen used it as a means to advertise or boost a separate enterprise. David Lewis, founder of Lewis's department stores (first in Liverpool and later in Manchester and Birmingham), started selling 'Lewis's Two-shilling Tea' in the 1880s. By buying straight from the tea ships at Liverpool docks, Lewis was able to offer affordable tea to his customers. Within three years of launching it, Lewis was selling about 20,000 lb of tea a week. When he opened his Birmingham store in 1885, he cannily placed the tea counter right in the centre of the ground floor where it would act as a magnet for tea-craving customers.

Savvy slogans, enticing offers and competitions, memorable packaging (including beautifully designed and, now highly collectable, promotional tea

Tin tea caddies were an effective means of promoting brand awareness and encouraging customer loyalty. This particularly attractive caddy dates back to the early twentieth century and features scenes from children's stories and nursery rhymes.

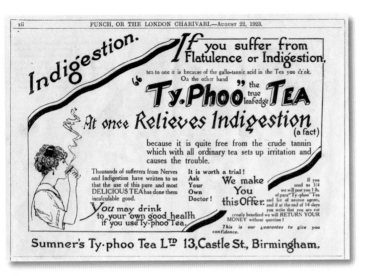

Ty·phoo claimed
that its tea had
special digestive
qualities and was,
accordingly,
successfully sold in
chemists across
Britain.

caddies) and colourful advertising all helped create recognisable brands.
Some companies, such as Co-op Tea, used dividends to stimulate customer
loyalty: on each packet was a stamp to be stuck on a card; when the card was
complete, it could be exchanged for a gift or money. A few companies went
to even greater lengths to get noticed. In 1894, Priory Tea used a hot-air
balloon to drop promotional leaflets over the streets of Birmingham.

An early
twentieth-century
postcard showing
gypsies enjoying
afternoon tea.

Right: Time for a tea break for a farm labourer who has been busy scarifying a field.

Below: This wonderfully realistic mid- to late-nineteenth-century painting by Matthias Robinson shows two ladies enjoying *A Gossip over a Cup of Tea*.

Those companies that had focused on developing a strong brand began to dominate the tea market. By the early decades of the twentieth century, these included Mazawattee, Brooke Bond, Co-op Teas and Ty·phoo (established in 1903 and famous for its 'one blend, one price' approach).

Both cheaper and more conspicuous, by the end of the nineteenth century tea was enjoyed at every level of a rapidly expanding population, from servants, gypsies, farmers and factory workers to the aristocracy and members of the royal family. Each had their own tea-drinking rituals and routines.

Perhaps the most significant tea-related development in the upper echelons of society was the introduction of afternoon tea in the early 1840s. With dinner moving later into the evening (from between 4 pm and 5 pm in the late eighteenth century to about 7.30 pm in the 1850s), there was now a need for an afternoon 'snack' to fill the gap between luncheon – a light midday meal – and dinner. Many historians attribute the appearance of afternoon tea to Anna Maria Russell, Duchess of Bedford and friend of Queen Victoria. After experiencing 'a sinking feeling' in the late afternoon, she realised that sandwiches served with cake and tea were the perfect antidote to her complaint. She invited friends to share her new habit and soon the wonderful British custom of afternoon tea was born. Scones were not a common feature of nineteenth-century afternoon teas; only in the twentieth century did they become such an intrinsic part of the ritual.

Queen Victoria, the inspiration for the famous Victoria sponge, enjoyed tea perhaps more than any king or queen before her. Her endorsement certainly helped establish the habit of taking afternoon tea, which by the 1860s had become widespread amongst the rich and by the end of the century was also common amongst the middle classes. The wealthy, again possibly inspired by the habits of Queen Victoria, were also fond of larger and more formal versions of afternoon teas, known as tea receptions and 'at homes'. These could cater for up to two hundred guests and usually took place between 4 p.m. and 7 p.m., during which people could come and go as they pleased.

Edwardian tea gowns often featured attractive lace inserts and allowed more freedom of movement than other more corseted dresses.

This portrayal of *The Wife at Home* appeared in *The British Workman* newspaper in 1863.

Tea was so much part of a woman's social agenda that by the 1870s tea gowns had started becoming fashionable. Made of light, flowing fabrics, these dresses were designed to be worn indoors in the intimate company of friends or family. They were less formal than day dresses or evening gowns and, being looser, much more comfortable as well. They may have helped bring about the more free-flowing shapes in women's dress that appeared during the early part of twentieth century. Tea gowns, albeit in different styles reflecting changes in fashion, remained fashionable until the 1950s.

While the rich had their 'at homes', the lower classes developed their own tea-drinking occasion. Although they drank tea during the day, the working classes had very little time to enjoy anything as leisurely as afternoon tea. When they returned from the factory, mine or fields in the early evening, what they needed was an invigorating meal to satisfy both thirst and hunger. This meal, which became known as 'high tea' and was usually taken at about 6 pm, featured cold meats, pies, cheese, potatoes, and bread or crackers supplemented by a pot of steaming tea. Why was it described as 'high' tea? A possible explanation may be that while afternoon tea was mainly enjoyed in low, easy chairs (and was sometimes known as 'low tea'), partakers of high tea would sit up at a table. Ironically, the rich developed their own more elaborate version of high tea – a perfect meal for times when servants were either at church (on Sundays, for instance), away or unwell. This type of high tea mixed ingredients from afternoon tea (cakes) with those of high tea (cold meats and pies) and extra luxuries such as pigeon, veal, salmon and fruits.

At the end of the nineteenth century, a major development was the appearance of tea rooms. The first tea room is said to have been the brainchild of a manageress working for the Aerated Bread Company (known as ABC). The story goes that while working at the ABC shop on Fenchurch Street in London, she started serving free tea and snacks to her best customers. This proved so successful that she asked the directors whether they would consider establishing such a practice on a commercial basis. They agreed and the first tea room was born. By the end of the century, there were at least fifty ABC tea rooms. Other companies followed their example, including Kardomah,

ONE OF THE TEA ROOMS

Art Nouveau ornamentation and furniture abound in this 1905 postcard displaying one of the elegant tea rooms at the London Coliseum.

Lockharts and the Express Dairy Co., but Lyons was without doubt the most successful. After starting life as a tobacco business in 1887, Lyons quickly branched out into catering. By 1894 the company had established a chain of tea shops – and, from 1909, Lyons opened its famous corner houses, more of these later – which were to become an important part of daily life for many British workers.

While tea shops and tea rooms sprang up across the country, Glasgow was a particular hotspot. As Perilla Kinchin explains in her book *Tea and Taste: Glasgow Tea Rooms 1875–1975*:

> The tea rooms filled a 'felt need', as their proliferation at the end of the nineteenth century shows. They were called into being by various things: by the strength of the temperance movement in the West of Scotland; by a native tradition of fine sweet baking; by the Scottish high tea; but most of all by the practical demands of a busy mercantile city.

Established in the 1830s, the temperance movement certainly had a strong influence – not just in Glasgow, but throughout the country. Temperance meetings, held across Britain, were designed to encourage people to swap beer, spirits and other 'intoxicating' drinks for non-alcoholic beverages by 'taking the pledge'. Tea, which was served during these reunions and at special 'tea festivals', almost became a symbol of temperance. As Prime Minister William Gladstone, himself a fervent tea drinker, once said: 'The domestic use of tea is a powerful champion able to counter alcoholic drink.'

This Art Nouveau silver caddy spoon was designed for Liberty and Co. in 1901.

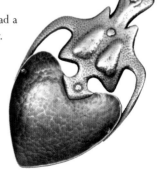

37

The two fashionable ladies in *Summertime: Afternoon Tea* (1889) by Rhoda Holmes Nicholls are enjoying what might be an impromptu cup of tea on the banks of a river.

A housemaid serving tea – but is the cup for herself or the photographer?

With their strong adherence to the temperance cause, many Glaswegians were ready for an alternative to the public house. This led to the opening, from the 1870s, of a string of wonderful tea rooms, the most famous of which are the Willow Tea Rooms opened in 1903 (and still running today) with splendid interiors by Scottish architect Charles Rennie Mackintosh.

What could be more pleasant than a woodland setting for enjoying afternoon tea?

Even the freezing weather – or the fear of slipping and breaking a leg – did not deter some nineteenth-century skaters from enjoying their favourite drink on the ice.

Tea rooms were just one choice of venue when going 'out to tea'. Department stores also had wonderful tea rooms, allowing shoppers to take a break and meet friends, and encouraging them to extend their time in the store. Hotels, too, created their own tea rooms, such as The English Tea Room at Brown's Hotel in Mayfair. Established over 170 years ago, it is one of London's very best – and most quintessentially English – venues for afternoon tea.

Strange as it may seem, tea played an important role in the emancipation of women. At a time when there were very few places a lady could enjoy a drink or a meal on her own or see friends outside the home, these new tea rooms offered a safe spot in which to go out without a male escort.

Tea drinking was not just an indoor pursuit. When the weather was fine, tea would be taken in the garden, or even in woods and orchards. The growing popularity of picnics led to the appearance of special portable tea sets, while in cities tea stalls offered workers a chance to grab a drink 'on the go'. Even in the winter, a few avid tea drinkers drank it 'al fresco' while enjoying a spot of skating.

MODERN-DAY TEA DRINKING

THE RISE in tea drinking continued unfettered in the early part of the twentieth century. By the early 1930s, and despite the high unemployment and destitution of the Great Depression, tea drinking reached its peak, with over 10 lb consumed per person per year, equivalent to an average of about five cups of tea a day.

In times of hardship, it seems that most Britons turn to tea for solace. This was certainly true of Gordon Comstock, hero of George Orwell's 1936 novel *Keep the Aspidistra Flying*. Impecunious and living in a grimy bedsit, Comstock finds comfort in secretly drinking cups of tea, which are banned by his despotic landlady.

For the growing numbers of people who could afford tea, there was a vast number of venues to choose from, the most popular and numerous of which were the Lyons tea shops. After opening its first tea shop in Piccadilly in 1894, the company became one of the first successful catering chains in the country, opening over two hundred tea shops in the capital alone. During the first half of the twentieth century, the Lyons name became synonymous with consistency of service and products as well as value for money. Its Nippy waitresses – smart young ladies clothed in a black dress with a rounded white collar – became an icon for the brand. The Nippy was used on advertisements, packaging and promotional items.

Rather than being the haunt of the rich and well-to-do, Lyons tea shops were particularly popular with the growing numbers of female workers, who were attracted by the clean, safe surroundings, not to mention the affordable teas and cakes and the simple hot food.

Lyons' tea shops and restaurants were often strategically located on busy streets in London and other large towns and cities. Situated at the junction of major roads, the Lyons Corner Houses were well placed to attract customers. One of the first to open was the Strand Corner House, established in 1915 at the intersection of the Strand and Craven Street. Sometimes as high as five storeys, Lyons Corner Houses employed about 400 staff, while orchestras – a different one on each floor – played continuously.

Opposite:
A French 1920s poster celebrating the fanciful idea of a 'tea promenade', during which travellers would be able to savour tea and cakes while enjoying glorious mountain views from a luxurious, chauffeur-driven car.

Right: The ground-floor Brasserie was one of three different eating areas at Lyons' Oxford Corner House.

THE BRASSERIE

LYONS' OXFORD CORNER HOUSE
Oxford Street & Tottenham Court Road, London, W.1.
Proprietors: J. Lyons & Co., Ltd.

Founded in Kensington in 1892, Fuller tea rooms were the ideal choice for tea drinkers looking for smaller, quieter and more elegant surroundings. As Claire Hopley, author of *The History of Tea*, explains, 'Friends met in cosy alcoves; tea came in elegant cups with beribboned tongs for sugar.' Other small tea-room chains opened across the country, including the famous and still operating Betty's of Harrogate, founded in 1919 by the Swiss confectioner, Frederick Belmont. Branches of Betty's later opened in other Yorkshire towns, such as York, Skipton and Ilkley.

Above: Lyons' Oxford Corner House opened in 1923. This photograph dates from 1931.

Right: The opulent lounge at the Prince of Wales Hotel located on London's De Vere Gardens played host to elegant afternoon teas, as this Edwardian colour postcard vividly captures.

Left: The Ritz's Palm Court is as stunning today as it was when Edward VII dined there in the early twentieth century.

Below: Brown's Hotel has been serving elegant afternoon teas in its English Tea Room for over 150 years.

Outdoor tea dances did not come better than those at Rushen Abbey's Dancing Floor and Tea Gardens.

The Waldorf Hotel's Palm Court, where guests could indulge in their love of dancing and enjoy a revitalising cup of tea.

All of them offered a choice of tea blends and a wonderful selection of ambrosial pastries and cakes.

Tea drinkers looking for even smarter surroundings could head for one of many grand hotels, such as the Ritz or Brown's, both in Mayfair, or the Savoy on the Strand. Today, the scintillating surroundings of the Ritz's Palm Court or the country house sophistication of Brown's English Tea Room still

tempt afternoon tea devotees. These days, however, one often has to book weeks in advance to be assured a table.

During the second decade of the twentieth century, the capital was gripped by a trend for 'tango teas', following the arrival in London of the tango, from Argentina via Paris, in about 1910. Responding to this new craze, some of London's grandest hotels held weekly tea dances, or *thés dansants*, as they were fashionably called. The most popular venue was the Waldorf Hotel, which hosted regular tango teas in its stunning Palm Court. Tables were placed around the dance floor and also in a viewing gallery above, where guests could sit down and enjoy a refreshing cup of tea between dances. In June 1913, *The Dancing Times* reported: 'The tango is graceful, decorous and worthy of a place in any ballroom. If you doubt me, go to one of the *Thés Dansants* organised by the Boston Club on Wednesday afternoons at the Waldorf Hotel, and you will be charmed.' The Savoy was also a popular venue for tango dances. Thanks to the enthusiasm of its tango-dancing manager, Sir George Reeves-Smith, tango lessons were available at the hotel. As the fashion moved from the tango to the Charleston in the 1920s, new music was incorporated into hotels' tea dances.

Far from being a solely indoor activity, tea dances were also sometimes enjoyed in specially designed tea gardens, such as those at Rushen Abbey on the Isle of Man. Tourists would flock to the island on charabancs to dance on the large wooden dance floor. Amongst the attractive gardens adorned with

Tewkesbury's extravagant Abbey Tea Garden, as it was in 1908.

Tables have been specially designed to wrap around the tree trunks at the Orchard Tea Gardens in Bossington, Somerset.

The tea rooms at Heacham in Norfolk, as photographed in the early twentieth century.

rambling roses, customers could delight in a cup of tea or a more substantial strawberry cream tea while listening to the orchestra and watching the dancing.

For those people not keen on dancing but still desirous to enjoy a cup of tea outdoors, there were many other options. A few London department stores created wonderful roof gardens where shoppers could take a break. Now sadly lost, the pergola-clad roof garden restaurant at Selfridges served morning coffees, lunches and teas. So too did the magnificent roof garden restaurant at the Derry & Toms department store. Now known as Kensington Roof Gardens, they are something of surprise on busy High Street Kensington and well worth a visit.

In towns, tea rooms or tea houses were a feature of public parks. In the countryside, the downstairs rooms of cottages were converted into tea shops, their gardens offering an idyllic spot for afternoon tea during the warmer months. A few orchards even doubled up as tea gardens, with restful deck chairs and low tables adding to the relaxed

atmosphere. The Orchard Tea Gardens in Grantchester near Cambridge are a particularly charming example. Planted in 1868, the orchard became a tea garden in the spring of 1897 after a group of Cambridge students asked the owner of Orchard House if they could have tea in the blossoming orchard, rather than on the front lawn. The idea was an instant success and since then generations of students have made the pleasant three-mile journey by foot or bike from Cambridge to Grantchester to enjoy a relaxing, rural tea.

When at the seaside, tea drinkers could choose from tea stalls or special beach-side tea rooms. Of course they could also, as was increasingly the case over the course of the twentieth century, bring their own teapot or Thermos flask.

Wherever you were and whatever your budget, you could now indulge in a 'nice cup of tea'. Even two world wars did not stop Britain from drinking tea. It has, in fact, been claimed that tea had a major impact on the outcome of the Second World War. Winston Churchill believed that tea was more important than ammunition. And in 1942, historian A. A. Thompson wrote: 'They talk of Hitler's secret weapon, but what about England's secret weapon – tea. That's what keeps us going and that's what's going to carry us through.'

A relaxed yet also refined seaside tea served from a gleaming teapot.

47

During the First World War, the Army Service Corps was responsible for getting food and essential supplies, including tea, to the troops.

During the First World War, people had to register with their grocer, who received an allowance of 2 oz per person per week. This quantity of tea would make an average of one-and-a-half cups a day. However, in *Liquid Pleasures: A Social History of Drinks in Modern Britain*, social historian John Burnett states: 'It seems that most people were able to buy as much as they wished, since families with large numbers of children did not take up the full allocations.'

Two days after the Second World War broke out the Government secured all stocks of tea and by 1940 it was rationed. The allowance was, once again, 2 oz per person (this time only for those over five years of age) per week. Those involved in essential work, such as firefighters and steelworkers, were given more, and, from 1944, anyone over 70 was entitled to 3 oz per week. During the Blitz, mobile canteens were set up on city

A Clarice Cliff Conical Early Morning Tea Set from about 1930. How one was supposed to pour the tea without the pot slipping out of one's hand is anyone's guess!

streets by the Women's Voluntary Service. Volunteers would hand out cups of tea and coffee and snacks to rescue workers and the thousands of people affected by the bombing. Even once the war had ended, tea continued to be rationed for another seven years.

The interwar years were a particularly innovative time for tea wares. After the First World War, more and more potteries focused on catering for the mass market. Companies such as Poole Pottery, Shelley and Susie Cooper created affordable tea sets with simple shapes and stylised decoration. Clarice Cliff produced some of the most memorable art deco tea sets. Perhaps her most wacky design was the Conical Early Morning Set, whose solid handles were virtually impossible to use comfortably. But what it lacked in

First produced in 1937, the Sadler Racing Car teapot is one of the most famous novelty teapots ever to be designed. Early models feature the number plate 'OKT42' (OK tea for two).

The English firm Wade, Heath & Co., who produced this Donald Duck teapot in the 1930s, was famous for its 'Disney Wadeheath Ware' featuring popular cartoon characters.

The Simple Yet Perfect teapot: its ingenious design allowed the tea to brew and then be separated from the beverage, thereby stopping the drink from ever becoming bitter.

practicality, it made up for in humour. Cliff's use of vivid colours, bold and often exuberant shapes and patterns were extremely popular, particularly between the wars. This was also the heyday of novelty teapots. Designed with fun firmly in mind, they came in every shape imaginable – from racing cars, trains, tanks and aeroplanes to Donald Duck, Humpty Dumpty, comical human faces and quaint country cottages.

Some novelty teapots were specially designed to offer an added practical benefit. Such was the case of the Cube Teapot, designed by Robert Crawford Johnson in 1919. Particularly suited for use on ships, and popular on liners such as the *Queen Mary*, it was guaranteed never to roll over during rough seas and was also easily stackable. Other innovations included the Simple Yet Perfect (or SYP) teapot, featuring an ingenious design with a built-in infuser shelf. The teapot was laid on its back for brewing. Then, once the tea leaves had infused for the necessary amount of time, the pot was placed upright: the leaves remained separate from the brewed tea, and therefore the tea never went bitter. Meanwhile, Lyons devised their own two-spouted teapot so that tea could be poured faster.

By the mid-twentieth century, such inventiveness started to spread into the electrical goods market. Although first produced in 1933 by the firm Goblin, the Teasmade had to wait until after the Second World War to make a real impact. It combined an electric kettle with an alarm clock enabling tea drinkers to wake up to freshly brewed tea. Like many other electric devices that became commonplace in the 1940s and later, such as washing machines and vacuum cleaners, the Teasmade helped replace the once almost ubiquitous housemaid of the pre-war years. By the 1960s, around 300,000 Teasmade sets were being sold each year in the United Kingdom; in the 1970s they came with an in-built radio.

One of the most significant tea-related developments to impact the second half of the twentieth century was the appearance of the tea bag. Like a few other great inventions – including, most significantly, penicillin – the origins of the tea bag were the result of chance. In the early twentieth century, New York tea dealer Thomas Sullivan created tea samples for his clients by placing small amounts of tea into little silk bags. Some mistakenly infused the bag, rather than taking the tea out of it first, and even went as far as reporting back to Sullivan that the silk was too fine and should be replaced by a different material. Soon Sullivan was producing specially designed gauze tea bags, ideal for infusing in boiling water.

The tea bag did not reach British shores until 1935 when Tetley added it to its range and even then it took a long time to catch on. By 1968 tea bags still held just 3 per cent of the British tea market. By 2000, however, the figure had jumped to 90 per cent. With the rise of the tea bag came the virtual demise of the teapot. Mugs, ideal for brewing a tea bag, became increasingly commonplace and almost completely replaced cups and saucers. Gone were the days of tea-drinking etiquette and ritual; now all that was needed was an electric kettle, a tea bag and some milk (poured directly from the bottle).

Punch, November 16 1949

Hawkins
Patented
Tecal
at your service

- Makes tea or coffee automatically while you sleep.
- Alarm wakes you when tea or coffee is brewed.
- The attractive reading-lamp lights to welcome you.
- "Smith's" Electric Clock gives correct time.
- Boiler switches off, leaving some hot water for shaving, etc.
- "Hawkins Tecal" is absolutely automatic and is fully guaranteed.

Patented Regd. Design

You'll praise the day you invested in TECAL.

If in any difficulty write to us for address of nearest stockist. Price £10.18.9 (inc. P.T.)

L. G. HAWKINS & CO., LTD. 30/35, DRURY LANE, LONDON, W.C.2

This wonderful contraption by Tecal combines a light, alarm clock and tea- and coffee-making device. As the advertisement explains, the alarm wakes you up when the tea or coffee is brewed.

A 1970s Twinings advertisement for Darjeeling iced tea. In the 1980s, iced tea became available in ready-made form, either in tin cans or plastic bottles.

Ice breaker.

Iced-tea with orange is a delicious drink to cool-off with at a party or barbecue, but first, you must choose your tea carefully.

Twinings Darjeeling, from the Himalayan foothills, is ideal because it has an exquisitely distinctive 'muscatel' flavour and is just as good chilled as it is hot.

Prepare the tea somewhat stronger than usual (a good rule to follow for any iced tea) and leave to stand for 5 minutes. Strain the tea into a large bowl with some crushed mint and leave to cool. When chilled, add 1 cup of brown sugar, the juice of 3 oranges, ¼ teasp. orange rind and plenty of ice.

Just before serving, fizz it up with a little lemonade and serve in tall glasses. Some guests may enjoy a drop of light, dry rum or a good brandy in this tea, but don't overdo it.

On every-day occasions, Darjeeling is served hot with milk and sugar according to taste. But taken without milk, you will find it is an excellent way to cleanse the palate after a rich meal of pork, goose or game.

Twinings Darjeeling is just one of our range of fine speciality teas.

Twinings Darjeeling tea.

Gone too were the days of fine teas or special blends; what most people wanted was a reliable and consistent 'quick brew' – the ideal beverage for an increasingly 'fast' and time-poor society.

Over the last forty years, the tea bag has evolved from square or rectangular sachets to circles and, most recently, pyramids. The argument is that pyramidal tea bags – also charmingly known as 'tea temples' – allow more room for the tea to brew and expand. Some tea rooms and tea aficionados also infuse fine teas in empty tea bags, featuring a top flap which folds down. Once the tea has infused for the right amount of time, the bag can be taken out of the teapot without the tea going bitter.

In the 1970s and 1980s, a trend for iced tea developed. Backed by an expensive television advertising campaign, Lipton started selling its ready-made 'Lipton Ice Tea'. Tea – at least in its 'iced' form – had joined the ranks of other convenience drinks sold in plastic bottles and tin cans.

The promoting of tea, like that of any other product, became increasingly elaborate over the course of the twentieth century. One of the most influential promotional tools ever used by tea companies were tea cards, inspired by the hugely popular cigarette cards, which had become available in the 1870s. Tea cards started appearing in Ty·phoo tea packets before the First World War, but it was only after the Second World War that the tea card craze really took off. It lasted until the 1980s. Collected mainly by children, tea cards covered a variety of topics, such as the history of the motor car, the race into space, exotic birds, trees, adventurers and explorers, wild flowers, dogs, cats, British costume, British kings and queens, and so on. For each topic, there was a set number of cards to collect and often an accompanying album in which to place them.

"Here, what's this? It smells like tea and tastes like cocoa!"
"Oh, that would be the coffee, Sir!"

Times have changed since this postcard, by famous graphic artist Donald McGill, was published in the 1940s. The British have developed a fondness for coffee and can now tell the difference between an espresso, latte and cappuccino.

Since the 1950s television advertising has played a key role in the promotion of tea. Together with the already mentioned Brooke Bond chimps, the Tetley Tea Folk were particularly memorable, appearing not just on our screens, but also on promotional tea towels, teaspoons, mugs, playing cards and tins.

Although tea has been facing increased competition from the coffee market over the last few decades, research into the health-giving properties of tea has helped increase the popularity of green tea, said to possess the strongest benefits. Even today, scientists are still making new discoveries into how tea can protect us from illness.

And while the majority of tea drinkers are still looking for convenience from their teas, the twenty-first century has seen a rise in the fashion for fine teas. Tea devotees are increasingly looking for good-quality, ethically produced and environmentally friendly teas, whether in leaf or tea bag form. And maybe a sense of ceremony has not entirely been taken out of tea drinking: after all, going out for afternoon tea – whether at a luxury hotel or in a cosy tea room – is still a popular pastime amongst the British.

Right: A striking example of Art Nouveau architecture and interior decoration, the Willow Tea Rooms in Glasgow were designed by Charles Rennie Mackintosh in 1903 and are still open today.

Below: The most elegant afternoon teas feature a choice of over thirty different teas, such as this one at the Lanesborough in London.

FURTHER READING

Burnett, J. *Liquid Pleasures: A Social History of Drinks in Modern Britain*.
    Routledge, 1999.

Faulkner, R. *Tea: East and West*. V&A, 2003.

Forrest, D. *Tea for the British*. Chatto & Windus, 1973.

Goss, S. *British Tea and Coffee Cups 1745–1940*. Shire, 2008.

Goss, S. *British Teapots and Coffee Pots*. Shire, 2005.

Griffin, L. *Taking Tea with Clarice Cliff*. Pavilion Books, 1996.

Hobhouse, H. *Seeds of Change: Six Plants that Transformed Mankind*.
    Macmillan, 1999.

Hopley, C. *The History of Tea*. Pen & Sword Books, 2009.

Kinchin, P. *Tea and Taste: The Glasgow Tea Rooms 1875–1975*. White Cockade,
    1996.

Macfarlane, A. and Macfarlane, I. *Green Gold: The Empire of Tea*. Ebury Press,
    2003.

Mair, V. H. and Hoh, E. *The True History of Tea*. Thames & Hudson, 2009.

Moxham, R. *A Brief History of Tea*. Constable & Robinson, 2009.

Pettigrew, J. *A Social History of Tea*. National Trust, 1999.

Tea, cake and the company of friends – who could ask for anything more?

TEA-TIME.
A seat prepared for some nice boy
O what a place for bliss and joy.

INDEX